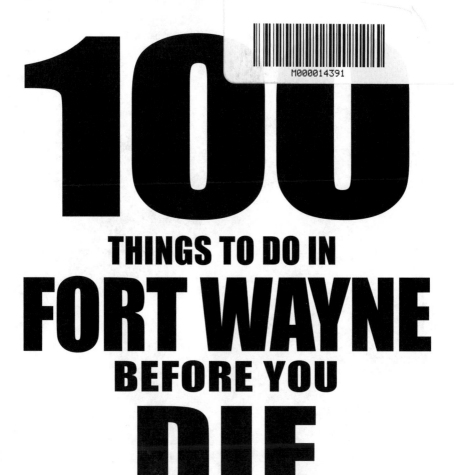

100

THINGS TO DO IN

FORT WAYNE

BEFORE YOU

DIE

100
THINGS TO DO IN
FORT WAYNE
BEFORE YOU
DIE

• •

TERRI RICHARDSON

REEDY PRESS

Copyright © 2021 by Reedy Press, LLC
Reedy Press
PO Box 5131
St. Louis, MO 63139, USA
www.reedypress.com

Library of Congress Control Number: 2021935154

ISBN: 9781681063188

Design by Jill Halpin

All photos courtesy of the author unless otherwise noted.

Printed in the United States of America
21 22 23 24 25   5 4 3 2 1

INTRODUCTION

There is a reason Fort Wayne has been named in a *Reader's Digest* article as one of the top 15 places to which to move. With a thriving arts and culture scene, fine dining, amazing parks and trails, diverse festivals, cool boutique shopping, and entertainment that fits whatever age or stage of life you may be in, it's a perfect place for the first-time visitor or the lifelong local. With so many options, you'll need some help picking which ones to experience. *100 Things to Do in Fort Wayne Before You Die* directs you to not only the tourist spots in the city, but also to those must-sees and must-dos that only those who live, work, and play in Fort Wayne know about. You can bite into a Coney dog that is a favorite of both locals and celebrities, or indulge in gourmet chocolates. Explore one of the country's top 10 zoos for children, see history at a replica soldiers' fort, or listen to top jazz musicians. Catch a minor-league baseball or basketball game, order a drink from a rooftop bar overlooking the city, or spend an evening touring downtown on a romantic carriage ride. This guide offers the top food and drink, live music and entertainment, culture and history attractions, sporting events, recreation, and shopping. All this, plus insider tips to get the most out of your time in the Fort, will make you want to keep exploring the city's offerings.

• •

CONTENTS

Music and Entertainment

Sports and Recreation

Culture and History

Shopping and Fashion

PREFACE

The last 21 years of my 30-year journalism career have been spent letting people know what there is to do, see, and experience in Fort Wayne. In that time, the city has grown into this quaint, cool, and ever-changing city, with a thriving arts and entertainment community and an amazing array of dining options that will satisfy the pickiest of palates. With so many things happening and new places opening, the city is constantly upping its dynamic.

Having come to the city as a transplant, I spent the first several years discovering what the Fort had to offer. Even after all these years, I'm still discovering new things and am constantly surprised at what I find. There are the best-kept secrets, such as the bowling alley in the basement of a church, the independent bookstore with floor-to-ceiling book offerings, or the public observation deck that overlooks a working rock quarry, and the favorites, like the science museum, children's zoo, and our minor league baseball team.

In *100 Things to Do in Fort Wayne Before You Die* I share these surprises, along with some oldies but goodies that will make your vacation to Fort Wayne one to remember. With so many things to do and see, you'll have more reasons to keep coming back.

It's the people and places in this book that have made Fort Wayne the best place to live, work, and play. I thank Fort Wayne's people for loving this city as much as I do and pouring their hearts into making it a welcoming place not only for visitors, but also for the people, like me, who call it home.

– Terri Richardson

ACKNOWLEDGMENTS

Thank you to all the people and businesses I have talked to over the years who have helped build the base of my knowledge of Fort Wayne.

Thank you to the teams at Visit Fort Wayne and Downtown Improvement District, who are the biggest cheerleaders and promoters of the city.

Thank you to my exploring partner, Scott. You were always willing to go with me wherever and whenever I asked. Your support is much appreciated.

And finally, thank you to my workplace, the *Journal Gazette*, for allowing me to take on this project and affording me the opportunity to continue reporting and writing about the city.

FOOD AND DRINK

HAVE A CONEY AND A COKE
AT CONEY ISLAND WIENER STAND

Stepping into Coney Island is like stepping back in time. It claims to be the oldest hot dog stand in America, having opened in 1914, and there's really no difference now from what it looked like then. Visitors can grab a stool and sit at the counter or at one of the tables and order what regulars know as "three and a bottle" (Coke, that is), which comes from the 1930s McCray cooler that's still in operation. Photos of celebrities who have come in for a dog dot the walls and are worth a mini-tour around the joint to see the who's who of Coney lovers. There's usually a line waiting to get into the restaurant, but your patience will pay off when you're able to bite into that juicy dog topped with Coney sauce and nestled into a steamed bun. Onions are optional.

131 W Main St., 260-424-2997
fortwaynesfamousconeyisland.com

TIP
You can stand on the sidewalk outside the downtown eatery and see the dogs lined up cooking on the grill from the front window that displays a "Coney Island" neon sign. It's a great sight at night.

DINE HISTORIC
AT THE GAS HOUSE

Located in the old city gas plant in downtown Fort Wayne, The Gas House is a unique dining experience that exudes historic ambiance. It can be as swanky or as simple as you want it to be. The longtime family restaurant is known for its upscale meals that range from steaks to seafood to hamburgers and salads. It's the perfect place for a business lunch or a night on the town. The best part is that the building also houses a second restaurant with a different theme. Upstairs, diners get a taste of culinary acrobatics at Takaoka of Japan, where chefs cook the meals on a hibachi grill right in front of you. While the meal isn't free, the corny jokes are.

305 E Superior St., 260-426-3411
donhalls.com/the-gas-house/

TIP

Party on the river during warmer months at The Deck, which sits along the back of The Gas House. The restaurant, overlooking the St. Marys River, offers a full bar as well as an outdoor dining menu to go with the watery view.

DRINK MOONSHINE
AT THREE RIVERS DISTILLING

The still at Three Rivers Distilling Company is something to see, which is just what the distillery team had in mind when it opened its doors. The giant, silver equipment is front and center in the building, which once housed a bakery—ideal for what's cooking there now. At Fort Wayne's only distillery, you can not only see where your drink is made, but also sample hand-crafted drinks such as moonshine, vodka, rum, bourbon, gin, or rye whiskey. The distillery offers tours and education about how the products are made, taking visitors throughout the production facility. For indoor dining, there is a restaurant and a private lounge overlooking the distillery, making it a perfect cocktail of dinner and drinks, set in the heart of downtown.

224 E Wallace St., 260-745-9355
3rdistilling.com

TIP
Travel the Northern Indiana Beer Trail, which includes additional breweries. Participants can sample craft beers, get a stamp in their passport for each visit, and land some cool swag along the way.
facebook.com/NorthernINBeerTrail

OTHER GREAT BREWERIES

Trubble Brewing
2725 Broadway, 260-267-6082
trubblebrewing.com

The Landing Beer Co.
118 W Columbia St., 260-265-2022
landingbeer.com

2Toms Brewing Co.
3676 Wells St., 260-402-7644
2tomsbrewing.com

Gnometown Brewing Co.
203 E Berry St., 260-422-0070
gnometownbrewing.com

Summit City Brewerks
1501 E Berry St., 260-420-0222
summitcitybrewerks.com

Fortlandia Brewing Co.
1010 Spring St., 260-424-2337
fortlandia.com

Mad Anthony Brewing Co.
2002 Broadway, 260-426-2537
madbrew.com

Hop River Brewing Co.
1515 N Harrison St., 260-739-3931
hopriverbrewing.com

Junk Ditch Brewing Co.
1825 W Main St., 260-203-4045
junkditchbrewingco.com

DINE FARM-TO-FORK
AT JOSEPH DECUIS

It is true that things taste better when they come straight from the farm, and the Eshelman family has taken that concept to the extreme with their fine-dining restaurant, located in a charming small town just 15 minutes from Fort Wayne. What started out as a place to feed business clients has been transformed into a culinary destination for everyone. From the food to the ambiance to the décor, every part of the restaurant is designed to create a unique dining experience. The restaurant offers a farm-to-fork concept, serving food grown from its nearby farm that includes vegetables and Wagyu beef. Joseph Decuis has been voted one of Indiana's best restaurants, as well as one of the top 50 restaurants in the country.

191 N Main St., Roanoke, IN, 260-672-1715
josephdecuis.com

TIP
While the food is worth the trip, the Joseph Decuis brand is really a destination experience, offering visitors the opportunity to buy its products and Indiana-sourced items in its Emporium, stay at its bed-and-breakfast in a historic home and farmhouse, or take a tour of the farm to see firsthand where the food is grown.

SIP HANDMADE SODAS AND FLOATS
AT LINCOLN TOWER SODA FOUNTAIN

Cozy up to the counter at the Lincoln Tower Soda Fountain, where old-fashioned fountains offer you a choice of several soda flavors. You can also add in some ice cream to make it a float. Located in a historic building that is more than 90 years old, the small shop truly is one of the city's best-kept secrets. While some things have been modernized, visitors still get a glimpse of those early days when busy workers would pop in for lunch. It's still a lunchtime favorite, as workers take their food to go or to a nearby stool at a table tucked in the back of the little shop. It's open only from 7 a.m. to 3 p.m. Monday through Friday.

116 E Berry St., 260-424-0030

TIP
The little soda shop is next door to the Lincoln Tower Bank, which allows visitors to walk in and view the art deco design. With beautiful high ceilings and ornate designs, it is a true sight to see. The building was once the tallest building in Indiana.

RAISE A GLASS
AT TWO-EE'S WINERY

Surrounded by 40 acres of vineyard and trails, Two-EE's Winery offers its guests a sipping experience with a touch of sophistication. Minutes away from the hustle and bustle of the city, it's a great place for those seeking a day or weekend getaway. Guests can sample wine in Two-EE's tasting room or step outside to enjoy the winery's spacious outdoor area. While the inside is impressive with its modern design, including a wall of windows that allow you to see the winemaking process, the best experience is enjoying a bottle, or two, of wine outside on the covered patio while watching the sun set over the gentle hillside. It's a relaxing scene that any wine lover will appreciate.

6808 N US 24 E, Huntington, IN, 260-672-2000
twoees.com

TIP
In addition to Two-EE's, Fort Wayne is surrounded by five other wineries just a short distance from the city. Visitors can make a day, or a few days', trip in visiting all of them.

OTHER WINERIES

Hartland Winery
425 County Rd. 23, Ashley, IN, 260-587-3301

hartlandwinery.com

Byler Lane Winery
5858 County Rd. 35, Auburn, IN, 260-920-4377

bylerlanewinery.com

Briali Vineyards & Winery
102 W Indiana 120, Fremont, IN, 260-495-1919

brialiwinery.com

Satek Winery
6208 N Van Guilder Rd., Fremont, IN, 260-495-9463

satekwinery.com

Country Heritage Winery and Vineyard
185 County Rd. 68, LaOtto, IN, 260-637-2980

countryheritagewinery.com

PARTAKE OF CONFECTION PERFECTION
AT DEBRAND FINE CHOCOLATES

These upscale gourmet chocolates can be considered edible art, created in the family-owned business with four Fort Wayne locations. Even if you are a chocolate snob, you won't be disappointed with the creations offered at DeBrand's. Whether filled with fruit, cream, or different spice blends, the chocolates almost look too beautiful to eat—almost! There's something for every chocolate lover, whether you are a traditionalist or an adventurist. However, chocolates aren't the only treats on the menu. I can vouch that the sundaes and hot chocolate are also must-tries. Come fall, there's always the popular giant caramel apples. But who are we kidding? You don't have to wait until fall to celebrate chocolate every month (or day) of the year.

10105 Auburn Park Dr., 260-969-8333
5608 Coldwater Rd., 260-482-4373
4110 W Jefferson Blvd., 260-432-5050
878 Harrison St., 260-969-8353

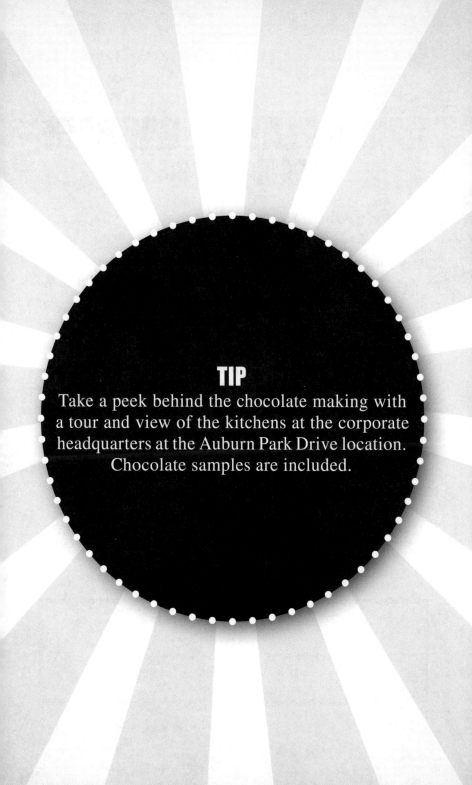

TIP

Take a peek behind the chocolate making with a tour and view of the kitchens at the corporate headquarters at the Auburn Park Drive location. Chocolate samples are included.

HAVE A PLATE OF GARBAGE
AT CINDY'S DINER

This '50s-style diner had several locations (four, in fact) around the city before settling at its current spot. It's not Cindy who will be serving up the greasy diner comfort food, but it's tasty all the same. You'll be rubbing elbows, literally, with other diners, as the restaurant can only serve 15 at a time. Its most famous dish is a plate of Garbage (hash browns, eggs, cheese, onions, and ham) for breakfast. However, it is also known for its burgers and its doughnuts, which are still made with the original doughnut recipes and a machine that came from the former Murphy's Five and Dime. Coffee, which goes great with a doughnut, is poured into one of the several mismatched mugs that hang along the wall.

230 W Berry St., 260-422-1957

TIP
Because the diner is so small, waiting for a spot at the counter is not only common but expected.

EAT, WALK, AND TALK
WITH FORT WAYNE FOOD TOURS

Fort Wayne Food Tours offers a chance to discover downtown, not only with the eyes but also with the stomach. Guided culinary walking tours on Fridays and Saturdays from May through September share not only the tastes of downtown restaurants, as participants travel to several locations to sample dishes, but also offer a lesson on the city's history and architecture. Restaurants are welcoming, and those on the tour receive interesting facts and tidbits about the city's past and present life. The 3.5-hour tour is about 1.5 miles and costs $60. The cool thing is that, whether you come alone or bring a friend, chances are you will meet several new people while walking, talking, and eating.

260-312-7343, 800-656-0713
Fortwaynefoodtours.com

TIP
Come hungry for the food and history.

FEEL BLUE
AT LA MARGARITA

Sometimes you just need to be festive. As festive colors go, blue isn't really the one you think of to brighten your day, but La Margarita's famous big blue margarita will definitely change your mind. The special margarita is one of the things the restaurant is known for and is a favorite among regulars. It's a perfect drink to imbibe alongside great Mexican dishes at this family-owned-and-operated restaurant. And don't skip the chips and salsa. The salsa recipe is a family secret and is known only to a handful of people. It's been made the same way for the last 50 years. In fact, many people come in just for the chips and salsa. Cooling down the heat of the salsa is one more reason to order the margarita.

2713 S Calhoun St., 260-456-5857

TAKE IN
BREWS AND VIEWS
AT CONNER'S ROOFTOP

Conner's Rooftop is the only open-air rooftop in Fort Wayne that overlooks the city's panorama. Located on the seventh floor of the Hampton Inn & Suites, it touts itself as a higher class of casual. But there's nothing casual about the views you'll get of downtown and the neighboring Parkview Field baseball field. If you time your visit right, you can even catch a game. Diners can gather around fire pits and order from a small bites and drink menu. It's a late-evening communal spot that doesn't open until 5 p.m. Conner's Rooftop doesn't take reservations, and space can fill up quick, so you should get there early to secure a spot, especially if you want to sit outside. And really, who wouldn't, with views like these?

223 W Jefferson Blvd., Ste. 750, (260) 702-0348
connersrooftop.com

TIP
Conner's Kitchen + Bar inside nearby Courtyard by Marriott accepts reservations and offers breakfast, lunch, and dinner.
1150 S Harrison St., 260-467-1638

ORDER A TEENY MARTINI
AT HT2 COCKTAIL LOUNGE

Martinis are big when it comes to cocktails, which may be why they are shrinking at HT2. Every Tuesday, HT2, or Hotel Tango, offers up mini versions of some of its well-known cocktails. The flights rotate flavors each week. Often it's seasonal flavors that are only around for a short time. The great thing about the martinis being smaller is it allows diners to try four different cocktails instead of one big one. It also allows for you to bring a friend (or a few) and share. Of course, just because you have four doesn't mean you have to share. Try all the flavors for yourself. And while cocktails are what it's known for, HT2 also serves wines and beers.

10212 Chestnut Plaza Dr., 260-616-0444

TIP
Looking for more places to imbibe?
Check out the menus for cocktail concoctions at:

Hideout 125
10350 Coldwater Rd., 260-206-6192
hideout125.com

Copper Spoon
301 W Jefferson Blvd., Ste. 100, 260-755-1019
copperspoonfw.com

GRAB A SLIDER AND A BAG OF CHIPS
AT POWERS HAMBURGERS

Powers Hamburgers is home to the classic slider and was named one of America's great original hamburgers by George Motz, considered to be one of the country's top burger experts. The small, white, art deco building with a striped awning has been in business since 1940. Stepping in is like stepping back in time. The bar stools around the counter fill up quickly, especially during lunch, as regulars come to eat in or place an order to go. The staff of the small grill works overtime to make the little sliders, which are topped with a heaping of grilled onions and with no fancy extras except ketchup and mustard. Expect to leave with a greasy bag, a bag of chips, and a smile.

1402 Harrison St., 260-422-6620

EAT THE WORLD
AT GEORGE'S INTERNATIONAL MARKET

If the goal of George's International Market was to create a world food tour, mission accomplished. Not only can you explore new cuisines from different countries, but a visit to the market is a cultural event in itself. The market, located in one of the most diverse neighborhoods in the city, offers meats, cheeses, and produce as well as homemade salsa and guacamole daily. Since Fort Wayne boasts many different ethnicities and immigrants, it has become a taste of home for many in the city. And whatever you do, don't skip the bakery. There are Mexican treats such as churros and flan, along with breads, cakes, and pastries. With so many choices, you may have to come back several times to try them all.

2021 Broadway, 260-420-5565
www.georgesinternationalmarket.com

TIP
Head next door to the Salsa Grille restaurant, which is owned by the same family that owns the market, and enjoy its tortillas and salsa bar.

SAVOR THE FLAVOR
OF CUPCAKES AT ZINNIA'S

When visitors come to the city, chances are they find their way to Zinnia's Bakehouse. Cupcakes at Zinnia's are big enough to share, but you probably won't want to. Each week the bakery offers different flavors, as well as other sweet treats such as macaroons, cookies, and scones. There is also a savory side to this sweet shop. Zinnia's makes empanadas and quiche. Everything is made from scratch, so once items are gone, they're gone. And be assured that items sell out quickly. Those in the know, know to check out the bakery's Facebook page or Instagram for updates on items being offered. While dropping in is not a bad idea, ordering ahead will ensure you get what you crave.

236 E Wayne St., 260-483-4765
zinniasbakehouse.net

TIP
The bakery is located inside a flower shop,
so street parking can be a problem.

TAKE SWEET NOTES
AT WEST CENTRAL MICROCREAMERY

If Willy Wonka owned an ice cream store, it would be the West Central Microcreamery. The only thing missing is the Oompa Loompas making the sweet, creamy goodies. The makers' combination of unusual ingredients are whipped into small-batch, handcrafted ice cream right in the store. Each flavor is given a quirky or clever name to describe it. Names include Philly Vanilli, Caught in the Rain (Piña Colada), You Down with OBB (Oreo Banana), and First Dance (wedding cake). The unexpected flavors (there's also vegan) just add to its uniqueness. The funky little shop is in a 94-year-old building located in the heart of downtown's West Central historic neighborhood. It's not a normal ice cream store, but why be normal when you're this good?

725 Union St., 260-214-2122
www.wcmicrocreamery.com

TIP

Time your visit with the annual West Central Home and Garden Tour, which takes place in September. The event allows visitors to see the interiors of historic homes, many more than 100 years old. The neighborhood was developed as a residential area during the city's canal era in the 1830s, and many of the city's most prominent families built homes there.
westcentralneighborhood.org

CHILL OUT
AT ZESTO ICE CREAM STAND

A sure sign of spring in the Fort is the opening of the Zesto ice cream stand. There are several Zestos in the city, but the one that stands out is the Broadway location, which has been in the same neighborhood since 1949. It's a landmark, serving its soft serve in cones, sundaes, and milkshakes to hundreds each year. The ice cream stand opens for business sometime at the end of March or early April and usually closes for the season after the first weekend in October. Never mind that the first frozen treat of the year may be served while it's still chilly outside. You'll have warm thoughts that summer is just around the corner with that first lick of the season.

2225 Broadway, 260-456-6298
5740 Falls Dr., 260-436-6531
6218 St. Joe Center Rd.
210 E Washington Center Rd.
zesto-ice-cream.com

ZOINKS!
ORDER SCOOBY SNACKS
AT MAD ANTHONY'S

It's no mystery that the Scooby Snacks at Mad Anthony Brewing Company is one of the most popular menu items. These potato wedges covered in Maryland crab seasoning have become a fan favorite in the Fort. However, this appetizer isn't the only thing served here. There are sandwiches, salads, tacos, and pizza. Mad Anthony's is a cool restaurant with a '60s vibe, located in what was the first Kroger store in Fort Wayne. The family dining area is known as the "Original" Munchie Emporium Restaurant, where the ceiling is covered in names of old-school patrons. And since this is a brewpub (the production brewery is located in the parking lot, and the original brewery can be seen through windows in the brewpub dining room), you can wash down those munchies with locally-made craft beers, ales, and lagers.

2002 Broadway, 260-426-2537
madbrew.com/fortwayne

TIP
While you're enjoying the craft beer and food, listen to live music from local bands. There's open mic night on Thursdays and scheduled tunes on Saturdays.

STEAK A CLAIM
AT OFFICE TAVERN

Ribeye steak is not usually considered bar food, but at Office Tavern there's nothing usual about the menu or the choice of meat. This neighborhood bar is known for its steaks—big, monstrous steak dinners that include rib eye and New York strip. The steaks are hand-cut and served in thick cuts of 16 to 18 ounces. The best part is that the steaks range in price from $15 to $17. It's an upscale meal at a good price. The bar also serves up some pretty good hamburgers and nachos. If you don't feel like cooking after a long day at work, Office Tavern is a perfect place to come unwind, order a steak, and have a beer to wash it down.

3306 Brooklyn Ave., 260-478-5827

TIP
The kitchen doesn't open until 5 p.m. and seating is limited, so get there early to snag a table.

GET YOUR GEEK ON
AT SWEETS SO GEEK

The force is strong with this purveyor of desserts, aimed to satisfy any geek's sweet tooth. It's one of the few places you can find chocolates in the shape of a Death Star or light saber from Star Wars, or a broom from Harry Potter. This quirky bakery has managed to combine pop culture and sweet treats by creating one-of-a-kind delectables. They truly know how to have fun with food. However, chocolates are just a small sampling of what's available. The store also has cookies, cupcakes, pies, and handmade ice cream. Need a cake? They do those, too. No matter what you order, you can bet it will appeal to the geek and the geek at heart—and it all comes from the minds of its equally geeky owners.

6722 E State Blvd., 260-312-5758
sweetssogeek.com

ENJOY HOOSIER FAVORITES:
BREADED TENDERLOIN AND SUGAR CREAM PIE

Want to eat like a Hoosier? Then there's no better way to get a taste of Indiana than ordering a breaded tenderloin and a sweet meal-ender of sugar cream pie—the state's top pie pick. There are many places in the city where you can order a breaded tenderloin, and everyone has their opinion about which place offers the best. However, if you want to get both, the Lunch Box Café is a good place to start. The little diner's breaded tenderloin really is as big as your head. It comes with one bun, but you can order another for 50 cents more. And I'm guessing you'll need more than two. Or, you may want to skip the bun altogether. Just make sure you leave room for the pie.

8814 Coldwater Rd., 260-490-5722
lunchboxcafefw.com

TIP

Just 20 minutes from Fort Wayne is the birthplace of the breaded tenderloin. Nick's Kitchen in Huntington is home to the original sandwich, which they have been making with the same recipe since 1908. Nick's is known nationally for its breaded tenderloin. It's also known for its pies, including sugar cream.

506 N Jefferson St., Huntington, IN
260-356-6618 nicksdowntown.com

GRAB A SEAT
AT CITY'S OLDEST BAR: OYSTER BAR

The Oyster Bar started out as a saloon in 1888, making it the oldest-known watering hole in the city. Now a seafood restaurant, it has remained in the same location for more than 130 years. Its specialty is not hard to guess: oysters. It has been reported that the restaurant goes through six to eight bushels of oysters a week (a bushel of oysters usually contains 100 to 150 oysters, depending on the size), prepared in various ways. The restaurant is dark and cozy, which adds to its charm but doesn't provide for a lot of seating. So, order a drink, along with some oysters, and toast to the fact that this bar survived the Frontier days, Prohibition, and the Great Depression.

1830 S Calhoun St., 260-744-9490
fwoysterbar.com

TIP
It's recommended that you make reservations before visiting, as seating is at a premium.

SWING WHILE EATING PIZZA
AT CLARA'S PIZZA KING

There really is no wrong way to eat pizza, is there? Which is why Clara's Pizza King makes it more fun to enjoy your pie by offering diners the option of porch swings to sit or swing on while eating. When you're ready to order that pizza, just pick up the old rotary-dial telephone on the table and ring the King to place your order. The swing and phones are just part of the whimsy of this restaurant that is two floors, is decorated with old portrait photos from floor to ceiling, and has a giant, stained-glass, oval window that overlooks the main dining room. The main star, however, is the pizza, cut into small squares, that will hit the spot no matter where you sit.

321 W State Blvd., 260-483-2163
9805 Illinois Rd., 260-800-3821
4226 Bluffton Rd., 260-747-1508
7203 Maplecrest Rd., 260-739-7624
305 State Rd. 930 E, New Haven, IN, 260-749-7337
pizzaking.com

GET LUCKY
AT DEER PARK IRISH PUB

If you're a lover of craft beer, then the luck of the Irish is with you at Deer Park Irish Pub. The pub offers more than 100 craft beers—not all of them Irish, but a great many of them are ones you've probably never heard of before. Just be prepared to get cozy with your fellow drinkers, as this watering hole is small and intimate. However, what it lacks in size, it more than makes up for in heart. That surely shows every St. Patrick's Day, when the pub hosts its holiday festivities, including the world's smallest parade. So, don something green along with your "Kiss Me, I'm Irish" badge, and plan to join in the fun in March.

1530 Leesburg Rd., 260-432-8966
deerparkpub.com

TIP
It's not Irish, but don't skip Deer Park's Taco Tuesdays.
They're not fancy, but come on, how can you go wrong with tacos and beer?

FEEL AMORE
AT ITALIAN CONNECTION

Dim lighting, intimate tables, and soft music make the Italian Connection a perfect place for a romantic dinner. With such great ambiance, you won't want to rush the evening. This family-owned restaurant fits the stereotype of those quaint and cozy Italian eateries you see in the movies. Family photos going back generations dot the walls, emphasizing the strong familial ties. Made-from-scratch dishes include handmade pasta and hand-rolled meatballs. Adding to the Italian charm, diners who come late enough can hear owner Alex Fiato serenade customers. Beginning about 8 p.m., Fiato pulls out the microphone and belts out a few tunes, and you can bet Frank Sinatra is among his favorites. It's enough to make any heart sing, "tippy-tippy tay, tippy-tippy tay."

2725 Taylor St., 260-432-9702

TIP
The restaurant is always busy,
so it's best to make a reservation to ensure you get a table.

GET SCHOOLED
AT SARA'S FAMILY RESTAURANT

Forget what you remember about school food. Although Sara's Family Restaurant is designed to look like a one-room schoolhouse, the dishes are way above anything that's served in a cafeteria. Bookshelves are lined with library books and metal lunchboxes, adding to the school décor. Diners can get a history lesson, as photos of every president hang around the restaurant, and part of the vast menu is dedicated to breakfast dishes named after our country's leaders. The restaurant's emphasis on presidents has also put it in the national spotlight as a site of national political visits, including the 2016 presidential campaign stop for Hillary Clinton. But there's nothing political about the decision to grab a meal at Sara's, and the only real debate will be what you'll order.

5792 Coventry Ln., 260-436-4185
sarasfamilyrestaurant.com

GO BACK TO THE FUTURE
AT RUSTY'S ICE CREAM

Dude! This ice cream store that's a throwback to the '80s is, like, totally tubular, for sure. Rusty's has bright colors, geometric shapes, tabletops dedicated to '80s films and albums, and a jukebox filled with '80s tunes. The best part is the ice cream, which is cleverly named such decade faves as Ninja Turtle, Pretty in Pink, Milli Vanilla, Rainbow Brite and Smurfalicious. You can throw on some ZZ Toppings to make it more special. Even if you don't remember the '80s, you will still enjoy the vibrant atmosphere. It's big and bold—everything the decade stood for. It's enough to make anyone want to breakdance. And here's a hint—for more '80s nostalgia, make sure you check out the bathrooms.

9171 Lima Rd., 765-969-1896
business.facebook.com/rustysicecream

MUSIC
AND ENTERTAINMENT

RING-A-DING-DING!
JAZZ IT UP AT CLUB SODA

Order a martini and slip into a seat to take in the cool sounds and sights at Fort Wayne's only jazz club. While you might not be part of the Rat Pack, it doesn't mean you can't pretend you're Frank, Dean, or Sammy and emulate the kings of cool. Club Soda features some of the best jazz and blues players in the region, which only adds to its hip factor. The restaurant bar has an extensive martini and cocktail menu, and the food is something to sing about as well. The menu boasts a number of culinary offerings, but the steak is the dish the restaurant is most proud of. It's a great place for an evening out or a late-night session.

235 E Superior St., 260-426-3442
clubsodafortwayne.com

TIP
Club Soda has live music Thursday through Saturday.

GO WILD
AT FORT WAYNE CHILDREN'S ZOO

The Fort Wayne Children's Zoo is a nationally-ranked zoo that offers a little something for the young and old. Visitors can spend the day exploring the 40 acres, filled with a variety of animals. You can feed the giraffes on the savannah or watch the lions prowl. Stand watch as orangutans swing in the rainforest and kangaroos lounge in the outback. Follow the sea lions as they put on an acrobatic show, swimming effortlessly by the visitors who pass the see-through tank. A giant aquarium features sharks and a large coral reef. The zoo also offers several rides and an animal carousel, not to mention opportunities to see some animals up-close and personal. And don't forget to visit Croaky, the joke-cracking frog that is a zoo legend.

3411 Sherman Blvd., 260-427-6800
kidszoo.org

TIP
The best time to visit the zoo is early morning or late afternoon, when the animals are the most active.

ENJOY OUTDOOR ENTERTAINMENT
AT FOELLINGER THEATRE

Foellinger Theatre is a unique entertainment venue that offers national, regional, and local acts in its open-air amphitheater. It's situated in a park, so you'll be enjoying whatever show you've come to see surrounded by nature. There's really not a bad seat in the house, as the theater is designed to give a great view of the stage, no matter where you sit. The theater has provided entertainment for more than 70 years, and thousands of people come to see performances each year. While many of the summer shows require paid tickets, the parks department also offers opportunities for free performances throughout the season. One of the more popular events is the summer movie series shown on a big screen when the sun goes down. The lineup is never typical, and that's what makes it a fan favorite.

3411 Sherman Blvd.
fortwayneparks.org

TIP
Performances take place rain or shine, hot or cold,
so make sure you dress accordingly and bring along some bug spray.

WALK THROUGH THE GARDENS
AT FOELLINGER-FREIMANN BOTANICAL CONSERVATORY

No matter the weather outside, the plants are always blooming inside the Foellinger-Freimann Botanical Conservatory. It's truly an oasis located in the heart of downtown. It's filled with indoor and outdoor gardens, so garden lovers can experience a treasure trove of flowers and plants in all different climates. Walking the paths can take you to a tropical rainforest with a waterfall, a desert full of cacti, or lush plants and trees you can't find in any city park. The conservatory offers different seasonal exhibits throughout the year. Some of its most popular are the live butterfly exhibit and the holiday display that includes Santa and live reindeer. Whether you're a visitor or a resident, the gardens offer a natural respite and give new meaning to flower power.

1100 S Calhoun St., 260-427-6440
botanicalconservatory.org

SMALL SPACE, BIG TUNES:
SETTLE IN AT THE BRASS RAIL

If there ever was a neighborhood dive bar, The Brass Rail would be it. Space is tight, but what it lacks in square footage, it more than makes up for with its live music from local and touring bands. The bar for many years has been rated the city's top venue for live music, which is offered most nights. That music can range from metal to punk to rock and even Latin soul. But whatever your musical tastes, you'll no doubt discover something to love about The Brass Rail. It could be the drinks, which range from bartender creations to craft brews and ciders. So plan to get cozy with the friendly crowd, raise a glass, and settle in for some great tunes.

1121 Broadway, 260-267-5303
brassrailfw.com

TIP
Be aware that parking could be a problem;
patrons may have to park on the street.

ROCK ON
AT SWEETWATER

The Sweetwater campus is a musician's paradise. With instruments to sample and buy, recording studios, several performance stages, and even dining options, there's no shortage of ways to find your own tune. Just as good as getting the gear, however, is using it to make music, and Sweetwater knows how to make the music. It offers free concerts on its indoor stage and national touring acts in its covered, outdoor performance pavilion. Sweetwater also offers clinics and workshops with well-known music producers and musicians offering their expertise, and the best part is they are open to anyone. Still looking for more to do? Well, Sweetwater keeps the entertainment rolling with an arcade and game room. It's a good guess that no matter what music you're making, Sweetwater can help you make it.

5501 US 30 W., 800-222-4700
sweetwater.com

TIP

Each summer, Sweetwater offers its annual music festival, Gearfest. It's a time when music lovers gather for performances and workshops from some of the biggest names in the music industry.

BE A HOLY ROLLER
AT MOST PRECIOUS BLOOD CHURCH
BOWLING ALLEY

In the basement of Most Precious Blood Church is one of the city's best-kept secrets: A bowling alley. The six-lane bowling alley, built in the 1930s, is operated by North Side Recreation Center. It was created as a way to help pay for the church, and has remained in use ever since. The bowling alley has an old-fashioned Brunswick automated pinsetter, not something found in today's modern facilities, as it's no longer made by the company. A concession area offers snacks and tables for eating, but you may want to bring your own shoes. The bowling alley is available for rent for parties and get-togethers, or to practice your bowling skills so you can get closer to that perfect score.

1515 Barthold St.,260-348-5346
preciousblood.org/bowling-alley

TIP
The bowling alley is in the church, which also operates as a school during the weekdays. So those wanting to use the recreation center should plan to do so in the evenings or on the weekends.

FEEL THE MUSIC
AT CLYDE THEATRE

The shows now playing at the Clyde Theatre are nothing like what was showing when it first opened in 1951 as a movie house. No longer showing classic films, the historic building has been transformed into an intimate music hall that stages national touring artists, as well as local and regional acts, from all different genres. Clyde Theatre offers live entertainment in a modern, state-of-the-art facility. Just be aware that once you score tickets to that performance, the show could be standing-room only—seats are not a guarantee and that's not because every show is sold out. The lack of permanent seating was a design choice—one of many that were made to make sure the entertainment experience is as good now as it was then.

1808 Bluffton Rd., 260-747-0989
clydetheatre.com

TIP

Once you score tickets, turn it into a dinner and show by heading next door for a meal or drinks at the Club Room. It does get busy on show nights, so reservations are recommended.

1806 Bluffton Rd., 260-407-8530
clydeclubroom.com

EUREKA!
EXPERIMENT
AT SCIENCE CENTRAL

If you never thought science was fun, well, it may be that you've been doing it wrong. Science Central makes learning about science enjoyable. It's located in the city's former power plant, which was refurbished to offer hands-on exhibits. Visitors can defy gravity on a bicycle 25 feet above ground, slide down a giant slide, or find out how a tornado forms. The Science on a Sphere exhibit demonstrates Earth and space, while another area allows children (and adults) to play in the water or see live animals. Everything from the multicolored smokestacks outside to the unique displays inside make Science Central a must-visit for all ages. With so much to see and do, you may not want to leave.

1950 N Clinton St., 260-424-2400
sciencecentral.org

TIP

Don't skip the hands-on demonstrations by staff, and check out the Science on a Sphere permanent exhibit, which has a giant sphere of the Earth that allows three-dimensional education about the Earth and space systems.

LISTEN TO THE CLASSICS
WITH THE FORT WAYNE
PHILHARMONIC

There is something elegant and sophisticated about attending the symphony. The fact that Fort Wayne has its own professional orchestra says a lot about the city's art and culture community. The Fort Wayne Philharmonic has been performing in the city for more than 70 years. The orchestra's full-time musicians are some of the most talented in the country, and perform hundreds of concerts each season. While each show is special, there are a few favorites that people look forward to each year. One of the symphony's most popular performances is its Holiday Pops, which takes place in the historic Embassy Theatre. The other is the Patriotic Pops, held around the Fourth of July, and usually at Parkview Field baseball park. The concert ends with a bang, culminating in a spectacular fireworks show.

260-481-0770
Fwphil.org

TIP
If you're worried about such things as what to wear to the symphony or orchestra etiquette, the Philharmonic offers a "what you need to know" on its website.

SEE WALKING DEAD TAKE OVER DOWNTOWN
IN ZOMBIE WALK

One day a year in October, downtown Fort Wayne looks like a scene out of an apocalyptic film. Thousands of people dressed as the undead fill the streets, moaning and groaning as they make their way along the roadway as part of the annual Zombie Walk. The walk is part of the Downtown Improvement District's Fright Night activities for Halloween. Participants—both young and old, including entire families—have fun with the event, some even donning elaborate costumes and makeup. Zombie makeup stations also are set up at the downtown library to help those who aren't that creative transform from alive to dead. But don't worry—the zombie mob only lasts a short time, and they are definitely not interested in brains.

260-420-3266
Downtownfortwayne.com/fright-night

TIP
The Zombie Walk is the kickoff of the Fright Night celebration, which offers other chills and thrills at various locations in the city.

GO SEE THAT INDIE FILM
AT CINEMA CENTER

Film lovers can find their community at Cinema Center. The independent movie house focuses on the art of film, offering independent, foreign, and documentary films that normally aren't shown at mainstream theaters. It has become a hub for movie watchers and moviemakers, often creating opportunities for both to discuss the film craft or delve into social issues during question-and-answer sessions after film screenings. Unlike in mainstream theaters, directors and actors in the films will show up to a screening here for meet-and-greets and to answer questions about the work. You won't find the big blockbuster films at this intimate theater, but you'll be entertained just the same. And you don't have to be a film snob to enjoy the types of movies shown here; you just need an appreciation for films and all that goes into making them.

437 E Berry St., 260-426-3456
cinemacenter.org

TIP

Each October, Cinema Center hosts Hobnobben, a film festival that features selected movies from diverse filmmakers both locally and worldwide. The event also offers film discussion, as well as meet-and-greets with the filmmakers.

FIND YOUR GROOVE
AT WOODEN NICKEL

Stepping into a Wooden Nickel store brings back the nostalgia of walking into a record store and flipping through multiple bins to find your favorite albums. Whether they be new or classic tunes, music lovers can lose themselves among the hundreds of vinyls, CDs and even cassettes at this independent music store, which has been around since the year MTV debuted. The staff knows about the music they carry, so if you know what you're looking for, chances are they can take you right to it if it's there. And if you don't know what you want, they can offer up suggestions based on what you like. But sometimes the fun is all in the hunt, especially when you discover something you have never heard before.

3627 N Clinton St., 260-484-2451
3422 N Anthony Blvd., 260-484-3635
6427 W Jefferson Blvd., 260-432-7651
woodennickelrecords.com

TIP

Fort Wayne is blessed to also have a second
independent record store, Neat Neat Records
and Music, which also offers the chance to
search for musical treasures in an eclectic space
not too far from the heart of downtown.
1836 S Calhoun St., 260-755-5559

CLIP-CLOP THROUGH THE CITY
WITH A CARRIAGE RIDE

I've done many things in Fort Wayne, but it wasn't until a few years ago that I took a romantic carriage ride with my husband through downtown. I booked with Sentimental Journey, one of three carriage tour companies that offers rides, and it was dreamy. The white carriage is pulled by a majestic horse, and the driver offers interesting tidbits and historical information about sites and buildings downtown. The tours are offered year-round, something to keep in mind around the holidays, when everything is aglow in holiday lights. Prices for most carriage rides range from $40 to $80 for a 30- or 60-minute ride. Most carriages seat up to four adults, so you could double-date or bring the kids. But I recommend keeping this trip a little more intimate.

Sentimental Journey
Ride starts at 305 E Superior St.
260-341-1133
sjcarriage.com

Other carriage rides:

Rosewood Carriage Rides
260-637-5261
rosewoodcarriagerides.com

Camelot Carriage Rides
260-223-2417
camelotcarriageride.com

TIP

Be aware that tours fill up quickly, especially near the holidays, so reservations are highly recommended.

SEE THE STARS
AT THE OBSERVATORY

It is often difficult to really see the stars in the city. But the Star*Quest Observatory makes it easy with its giant telescope, which is in a park set in an area away from the big lights of downtown. The best part is it is free. The observatory is operated by the Fort Wayne Astronomical Society and offers viewings with its telescopes every clear Saturday night from April through November, one hour after sunset, for up to two hours. It can be an amazing educational opportunity for adults and children, or it can just give you a chance to see the moon, stars, and planets in a different way. It also is an idyllic way to spend a warm summer night, staring up at the stars. Just make sure you bring some bug spray.

Jefferson Township Park
1720 S Webster Rd., New Haven, IN
fortwayneastronomicalsociety.com

TIP
Bring your own telescope, and trained volunteers will help and offer tips on how to use it more effectively. Also, other stargazers will willingly share their telescopes for additional viewing.

VISIT OLD SAINT NICK
ON THE SANTA TRAIN

Sorry, Rudolph and the rest of the reindeer, Santa won't need you for this special holiday trip. Every December, Santa parks his sleigh and boards the Fort Wayne Historical Society's Santa Train to offer a meet-and-greet with other riders. The trip with the Big Guy has been a holiday favorite for more than 20 years. The station turns into "Santa's Workshop," which provides visitors a chance to see railroad memorabilia, as well as the ability to climb aboard and explore historic steam engine No. 765, one of a handful of steam engines that still operates. The Santa Train is offered only for three weekends in December, which gives Santa plenty of time to get back in the sleigh to deliver those gifts on Christmas Eve.

15808 Edgerton Rd., New Haven, IN, 260-493-0765
fortwaynerailroad.org

TIP
Rides sell out quickly, so plan to book early. Visit the website in November or sign up for emails to learn when tickets go on sale.

RAISE YOUR VOICE
AT LIBRARY'S ROCK THE PLAZA

Rock the Plaza is one of the few times that you don't have to be quiet at the library. In fact, being loud is encouraged. Every Saturday during the summer, the main branch of the Allen County Public Library turns into an urban concert venue. Outdoor performances by local and regional bands reverberate throughout downtown and draw hundreds of people to the plaza. Multiple bands perform each Saturday, so the audience can hear a variety of music. Forget about buying a ticket, as all the performances are free. Concerts usually happen from June through August. There is plenty of parking in the library's underground parking garage or adjacent lot, or you can park along the streets.

900 Library Plaza, 260-421-1200
facebook.com/ROCK-the-Plaza-152763481460399

TIP

The concerts are on the outdoor plaza of the library, and seating is not available. It's suggested that you bring your own chair or blanket.

YOU GLOW, GIRL (OR BOY)
AT CRAZY PINZ

Golfers won't have to worry about losing their balls at the mini golf course at Crazy Pinz. That's because everything is aglow under its black lights. In addition to the golf course, the massive entertainment center also includes an arcade, a bowling alley, a rope-climbing course, laser tag and a rock wall. There are still the usual kitschy obstacles most mini golf courses have, but all are glow-in-the-dark and tucked into a cave-like structure that only adds to the fun. It is family-friendly, but if you are looking for a late-night activity for the adults, come back after the kids' bedtime. The course stays open to 1 a.m., so teeing off at midnight is not out of the question.

1414 Northland Blvd., 260-490-2695
crazypinz.com

TIP
The bowling lanes also feature glow-in-the-dark party lights.
Then, after 5 p.m., the black lights come on.

SKIP THE BROWN BAG
FOR LUNCH ON THE SQUARE

The lunch hour has never tasted or sounded this good. Each Thursday during summer, downtown's Freimann Square plays host to Lunch on the Square, offering a variety of food trucks, live music, and other activities. From June through August, a different band or musician performs on the plaza each week. Office workers and anyone else needing a break from their daily activities mingle during the two-hour event, with an opportunity to buy lunch (or bring their own) and settle in to listen. With so many food trucks, you'll have a hard time deciding what to order. It is a chance to escape the mundane and have a portable picnic outside, instead of sitting at your desk or the office break room with a Tupperware dish of leftovers.

200 E Main St.
downtownfortwayne.com/events/lunch-on-the-square/

TIP
Lunch on the Square isn't the only place to find local food trucks. You can keep up with their locations by visiting the individual trucks or going to Fortwaynefoodtrucks.com.

SEE HOLIDAY CREATIONS
AT FESTIVAL OF GINGERBREAD

These are no half-baked confectionery creations. Each holiday season, local artists use their talents to make elaborate gingerbread works to display at the History Center during the Festival of Gingerbread. It is an annual Christmas tradition and a holiday favorite that allows visitors to ooh and ahh over the gingery models made by artists of all ages and all skill levels. Participants spend weeks planning, baking, and decorating their creations to be a part of the festival. It will put you in the mood for the holidays, and may even make you want to try your hand at making a gingerbread house yourself. Just keep in mind that at the festival the houses are for looking only—sadly, eating is not allowed.

302 E Berry St., 260-426-2882
fwhistorycenter.org

TIP
It goes without saying that the festival is busier on the weekends, so if you want to spend more time lingering in front of your favorite gingerbread creation, try visiting on a weekday.

SPORTS
AND RECREATION

PLAY BALL:
FORT WAYNE TINCAPS BASEBALL

There is just something about opening day of baseball. For spring in the Fort, it means the first TinCaps game. Baseball fans are lucky to have a minor league team located in the city. The team, a Midwest League affiliate of the San Diego Padres, plays its games from April through September in the state-of-the-art Parkview Field stadium downtown. However, a TinCaps game is more than baseball. You may want to come hungry, as the stadium offers a number of concession stands with different food options that can be as basic as a hot dog or popcorn, but also include walking tacos, Italian sausage and apple dumplings with ice cream. Games offer family-friendly activities, with Johnny the mascot leading the crowd. And since ticket prices are so low, it becomes an affordable entertainment option—a home run for everyone who attends.

1301 Ewing St., 260-482-6400
milb.com/fort-wayne

TIP

When the TinCaps don't have a game, the ballpark is open for visitors to walk around the concourses, sit in the stadium seats and enjoy eating their lunch, or just think about the next game.

SKATE LIKE A GIRL:
FORT WAYNE DERBY GIRLS

This ain't no casual skate group. With players who go by names like Madame Furie, Kerr-Pow and Death Perception, you know the Fort Wayne Derby Girls mean business. This kick-butt group of women is Indiana's first all-female, flat-track, roller derby team. They travel all over the country and Canada to compete. And this is serious competition, so there's real contact made out on the track. Make no mistake that every time they slip on a pair of skates, they take their hits, as well as give them. But these women also have a soft spot. Every derby match helps the team raise money for women and children's charities. Since they first began in 2005, the Derby Girls has raised thousands of dollars for various good causes.

Matches take place at Memorial Coliseum, 4000 Parnell Ave.
usually from February through April
fortwaynederbygirls.com

TIP
Never been to a roller derby match? The team's website gives first-timers a crash course on the lingo and what is happening during the game.

BIKE, RUN, OR WALK
THE RIVER GREENWAY

The River Greenway Trail is a 25-mile trail system that winds throughout Fort Wayne, connecting with neighboring cities and counties. The trails offer beautiful, natural scenery and scenic overlooks, all situated in an urban environment. Many of the trails are along the banks of the city's three rivers – the St. Marys, St. Joseph, and Maumee. And depending on where you go and which trail you take, you can expect to see wildlife, including deer and various birds. The trail is open year-round, which means you get to see an amazing display of the seasons. No matter if you are using the trails for fitness, recreation, or conservation, they are a true asset that allow you to see the natural beauty of the city.

Fwtrails.org
fortwayneparks.org/trails/rivergreenway.html

WATCH THRILL RIDES
AT BMX TRACK

Bicycle motocross (BMX) can get your adrenaline pumping. As soon as the gate falls, BMX racers hit the track to navigate the obstacles, giving spectators a chance to see big jumps and high speeds. The bicycle motocross is in Franke Park and takes place on a primarily dirt track that is filled with hills, dips, and sharp turns that only add to the thrill of watching the sport. Each season, the track shakes up its obstacles for the racers, such as adding a four-dip straightaway called the "Quadzilla." Racers, who include both adults and children, come from several different states to compete. Races usually take place Wednesdays and Friday evenings from summer through fall. There isn't a large parking lot outside the BMX facility, so you should expect to walk a short distance to get to the track.

3411 Sherman Blvd.
usabmx.com/tracks/1752

ICE OUT, BABY:
HEADWATERS ICE SKATING RINK

What screams winter more than ice-skating? Whether it is a first date, 100th date, friends hanging out, or a family outing, head to Headwaters Ice Skating for a chance to take some turns on the covered, outdoor rink located in downtown's Headwaters Park. Each season, thousands of people flock to the rink, which is open from November through early March. You can bring your own skates, but ice skate rental is also available. Make sure to bundle up and bring some extra money for a cup of hot chocolate, because Indiana weather can be brisk and brutal at times. And remember, while it costs to skate, watching your family and friends take those icy falls is always free.

333 S Clinton St., 260-422-7625
fortwayneparks.org/facilities/headwaters-park-ice-arena.html

BECOME STONE COLD
LEARNING TO CURL

Curling is one of the most popular but puzzling sports to watch during the winter Olympics, but surprisingly, it does not take that long to learn. To master it, well, that is a different story. However, if you are willing to put in the effort, and most definitely to take a few falls, you can get started with Learn to Curl sessions at the Fort Wayne Curling Club. Sessions are offered twice monthly and will help you learn the art of the sport, from delivering the stone to sweeping. The club is open from mid-September through mid-April and offers leagues and competitions. And while you may not make it to the Olympics, all that practicing may help you do well in the next bonspiel.

3837 N Wells St., 260-739-5182
fortwaynecurling.com

FUHGEDABOUT CENTRAL PARK,
TRY FRANKE PARK

Franke Park's 339 acres may be a bit smaller than Central Park, but like New York's most famous green space, Franke is its city's largest urban park and offers a multitude of recreational activities. The park's property includes an outdoor theater for concerts, a zoo, a playground, trails, a BMX track, a lake for fishing, and plenty of places to have a picnic. If you are a hiker or mountain bike rider, the trails will really get you going. Dotted with large-rooted trees, creeks, and small hills, the various trail paths offer something for both the beginner and the seasoned veteran. For bicyclists, the trails have been touted as some of the best in the area for mountain bike riding.

3411 Sherman Blvd.
fortwayneparks.org/38-parks/park-page-links/168-franke-park.html

EXPLORE THE RIVERS
BY CANOE AND KAYAK

Since Fort Wayne was built at the confluence of three rivers
—St. Marys, St. Joseph and Maumee—it only makes sense
to stick a paddle in the water and explore the city by canoe or
kayak. Traveling along many of the water trails offers a unique
perspective of the city. The use of the rivers by canoers and
kayakers has increased over the years, so expect to pass many
friendly faces as you make your way along one of the waterways.
There are several boat launches positioned around the city that
will get your equipment into the water, but if you don't have your
own canoe or kayak, you can always rent one from Fort Wayne
Outfitters and Bike Depot or Earth Adventures Unlimited.

Fort Wayne Outfitters
1004 Cass St., 260-420-3962
fwoutfitters.com

Earth Adventures Unlimited
1804 W Main St., 260-424-1420
earthadventures.com

TIP
Not sure where to start or go on your kayak or canoe trip? Fort Wayne
Outfitters offers paddle trips on several of the city's water trails. Trips
take place on Saturdays and can be booked by calling 260-420-3962.

· ·

GET FIT
BY RUNNING OR WALKING
FORT4FITNESS

Who said getting healthy had to be boring? The Fort4Fitness Fall Festival is seriously the biggest celebration of fitness in the area. Thousands of athletes and non-athletes gather downtown each September to take part in the Fort4Fitness race. The race offers various events, such as a 4-mile, 10K, half-marathon, and Triple Crown, for all ages. What makes the event even more fun is that many of the racers—some alone, some in groups—dress in costumes or other matching outfits. And even before you cross the finish line, expect to be cheered on by groups of residents in the neighborhoods, many of them historic, that the race route winds through. The race culminates with a big party, where people can toast each other with a box of chocolate milk.

260-760-3371
Fort4fitness.org

TIP

You don't have to be a runner or walker to take part in Fort4Fitness. You can join the spectators who gather along the city streets for a block watch party. Since the race winds through several neighborhoods, associations gather to cheer the participants with signs, drinks, and even live music.

SIT COURTSIDE
WITH MAD ANTS BASKETBALL

Indiana and basketball go hand in hand. That's why it's a slam-dunk for Fort Wayne to have the Mad Ants basketball team make its home here. The team is the NBA G League affiliate of the Indiana Pacers. Games take place at the spacious Allen County War Memorial Coliseum. And while there are plenty of fans cheering for this team, they aren't the only ones. Part of the Antertainment includes the Fort Wayne Mad Dancerz, who keep the crowd going during home games, and the Mad Ants Drummers. After all, every sports team should have its own musicians, and these drummers bring the noise at each game, especially if there's a victory.

Allen County War Memorial Coliseum
4000 Parnell Ave., 260-469-4667
fortwayne.gleague.nba.com

TIP
Since the games are played at the Memorial Coliseum,
expect to pay a separate fee for parking.

CHILL OUT
WITH KOMETS HOCKEY

Every fall, hockey fans ready their coats, hats, and mittens to sit rinkside as the Komets take to the ice. The minor league hockey team with the East Coast Hockey League (ECHL) has a longstanding history in the city that dates to the 1950s. The number of championships the team has won over the years is quite impressive, and the team has earned a huge fan base. The games offer non-stop action, and yes, you will no doubt see a few fights once the puck is dropped and the gloves come off. You also will see Icy D. Eagle, the beloved mascot and face of the Komets. Icy keeps the crowd entertained with his hijinks, both on the ice and off, and his constant provoking of the other team.

Home games held at Allen County War Memorial Coliseum
4000 Parnell Ave., 260-483-0011
Komets.com

STOP AND SMELL THE ROSES
AT LAKESIDE PARK

A walk in the park never smelled so good. Gardeners and non-gardeners will appreciate this beautiful park, which features reflecting pools and a unique sunken garden with more than 2,000 rose plants of at least 150 different varieties. The park was named a National Rose Garden in 1928 and still holds that honor. It shouldn't be a surprise that the park is a popular place for weddings because of its scenic backdrops and fountains, but what happens in April and May is a little unexpected. Those months are prom season in the area, and during this time hundreds of high school students often descend on the park on Fridays and Saturdays for prom pictures. Why roses, you might ask? Well, apparently roses do very well in clay soil, which is what you get in Indiana.

1401 Lake Ave., (260) 427-6000
fortwayneparks.org

TIP
After you've smelled the roses, you can tiptoe through the tulips at Foster Park. The park is a great place to be in the spring, when the multitude of colorful tulips bloom. 3900 Old Mill Rd.

TEE UP
AT CITY GOLF COURSES

Golf junkies will find more than 30 public and private golf courses in the city. The problem will be deciding which ones to visit. The municipal courses located in city parks are a great option, with challenging and unique courses located among wooded backdrops and natural barriers. There's no better example of this than at Foster Park Golf Course. Foster Park may be one of the top courses, with 18 holes and a par of 71. Each hole is close together on this easy-to-walk course. You will no doubt use every club in your bag by the time you finish. Another plus with city courses is that fees are low, allowing you to spend that extra cash on golf balls. Course descriptions and prices are available at fortwayneparks.org

Foster Park Golf Course
3900 Old Mill Rd., 260-427-6735
fostergolfcourse.com

McMillen Park Golf Course and Driving Range
3900 Hessen Cassel Rd., 260-427-6710
mcmillengolfcourse.com

Shoaff Park Golf Course
6401 St. Joe Rd., 260-427-6745
shoaffgolfcourse.com

EXPERIENCE NATURE
AT WETLANDS NATURE PRESERVE

You never know what you might see along the 14 miles of trails through Eagle Marsh, an 831-acre wetlands nature preserve. Varied habitats include shallow wetland, sedge meadow, prairie, and mature forests. That's good news for hikers, who can view amphibians, wild animals, and birds, including nesting bald eagles. The preserve is protected and was restored by the Little River Wetlands Project, which gives tours, classes, and hikes at the preserve all year round. One of the more communal hikes is the Little River Ramblers, which is held on Tuesday mornings. When you do come, you might want to bring your binoculars and do some bird-watching. The preserve has recorded more than 250 bird species and is one of the suggested spots on the Indiana Birding Trail.

6801 Engle Rd., 260-478-2515
lrwp.org

TIP
The northeast Indiana area has other spots listed on the Indiana Birding Trail. You can check them out at indianabirdingtrail.com.

GO DOWN BELOW:
UNDERGROUND ROCK CLIMBING

When you think of rock wall climbing, it is usually not in a basement of a building. However, that's exactly where Earth Adventures Unlimited's climbing wall is located. Called the Boulder Down Under, the bouldering gym is often used by local rock climbers to help stay in shape in the off-season. Considering Fort Wayne doesn't have any mountains to climb, the rock wall will have to do. The great part is, you don't have to be a rock climber to use the wall. Luckily for adventure seekers, the Boulder Down Under is open to everyone, if you throw down a couple bucks and sign a waiver. The bouldering gym is usually used by rock climbers, so call ahead and make sure it is available for use.

1804 W Main St., 260-424-1420
earthadventures.com

TIP
Hours: 10 a.m. to 6 p.m. Tuesday through Friday
and 10 a.m. to 4 p.m. Saturday.

GET THE WHEEL DEAL:
WOODEN-FLOOR ROLLER-SKATING

There is just something about roller-skating on a wooden floor that takes you back to the 1970s, when skating was king and disco was its theme music. Bell's Skating Rink has been in operation longer than that, since 1926, and it has become a favorite place for family fun, with such events as $1 skate nights and family skate days. Don't worry if you can't skate very well, because Bell's offers skating sessions throughout the week. And while Bell's still has the wooden floor, it certainly doesn't have that '70s vibe. The DJ spins modern tunes as you make your way around the floor. But you can always revel in nostalgia by throwing on some bell-bottoms, adding fluffy poms to your skate laces and doing the hustle. Just know you'll probably be doing it alone.

7009 Indiana 930, New Haven, IN, 260-749-8214
facebook.com/BellsRink

TIP

You can also lace up your roller skates at
Roller Dome North. After taking a few laps
around the rink, doing the chicken dance, or
playing limbo, you can take a break and check
out the arcade and laser tag.
444 W Coliseum Blvd., 260-483-6303
rollerdomenorth.com

BECOME A PINBALL WIZARD

You can't do anything for 25 cents these days, especially when it comes to weekend entertainment. That changes at Fort Wayne Pinball Wizard's World Arcade, where a pocketful of change turns into an evening of fun. Playing the silver ball is what it is all about here. The arcade features about 80 pinball machines, some of which are more than 50 years old. Even if you have never played pinball, there is no judgment here. Rest assured that you are not the only person whose ball slipped past the flipper all three times in a matter of minutes. The good news is, you're not wasting a great deal of money if you lose. At just a quarter or two per game, you can give it a try and most likely find a machine that will make you flip.

14613 Lima Road
fortwaynepinball.com

TIP

Don't worry if you don't have a bunch of quarters; just like any good arcade that wants to make sure you are plunking money into the machines, Fort Wayne Pinball Wizard has a change machine.

PARK IT
AT PROMENADE PARK

Talk about a park with personality. Promenade Park is the newest addition to the city's green spaces and sits along the convergence of the three rivers—St. Marys, St. Joseph, and Maumee—in the center of downtown. The riverfront urban park is a spot for concerts, entertainment, and exploration, and is a good place to take a lunch break. A kids' canal with a running stream has giant rocks that kids can jump or sit on while splashing in the water. Seating built into the grassy hillside leads to a river walkway, and concrete games such as cornhole and foosball are positioned around the park. Make sure to walk along the Tree Canopy Trail, which connects to the historic Wells Street Bridge and leads to a playground on the back side of the park.

202 W Superior St., (260) 427-6000
fortwayneparks.org

TIP
Since the park is located downtown, parking is a little hard to come by, especially on the weekends. There is a parking lot next to the park, as well as on-street parking, but both fill up quickly. If you can't get there early, try parking a short distance away and walking to the park.

MAKE THE MOST OF A SNOW DAY
CROSS-COUNTRY SKIING

Fort Wayne may not have mountains for downhill skiing, but that doesn't stop residents and visitors from finding places to cross-country ski. The frequent heavy snowfalls in the area turn the hiking trails in two of the county's parks into the best places for cross-country skiing. The trails may be easy to tackle without the snow, but throw on the powder and skiers are sure to get a good workout. The trails also wind throughout the parks, which gives skiers a chance to experience nature in the winter. Four or more inches of snow is needed for the trails to be open for skiing. Equipment, though limited, is available for rental.

Metea County Park
8401 Union Chapel Rd., 260-449-3777
allencountyparks.org/parks/metea

Fox Island County Park
7324 Yohne Rd., 260-449-3180
allencountyparks.org/parks/fox-island

TIP
Find out ski conditions at allencountyparks.org.
A stoplight system tells skiers if conditions are good for skiing.

SEE A SUMMER HAZE OF SUNFLOWERS
AT THE FARM

Toward the end of August, rows upon rows of sunflowers tower over a field at Salomon Farm. The sunflowers, which stand at attention to face whichever way the sun is shining, offer a magical maze of summer beauty. Visitors can walk along pathways set among the maze of flowers, happily getting lost in their shadows. Bring a camera or carry a cell phone. It should be noted that snapping photos and selfies along the way is encouraged, and the park provides some staged photo opportunities just for the occasion. You may want to plan several trips to the sunflower field to ensure you catch the flowers at their peak. But don't wait too long to get there, as the flowers, like summer, don't last long.

817 W Dupont Rd., 260-427-6790

TIP
Salomon Farm also offers other ways to enjoy nature, including its trails and bird-watching, as well as a glimpse of life on a historic farm with its many animals, including ducks, chickens, sheep, and goats.

VIEW NATURE
AT AREA PRESERVES

With names like Bicentennial Woods, Cypress Meadow, and Fogwell Forest, a visit to an ACRES Land Trust nature preserve will make you feel like you just stepped into the pages of a storybook. ACRES Land Trust has made it its mission to turn donated land into preserves and trails that are free for public use. Each of the preserves is unique, offering sightseers a chance to walk among wildflowers and towering trees, wade in creeks, and see waterfalls and cliffs that have been carved out by water. Many of the preserves are still relatively undiscovered places, so you may be the only soul exploring them on most days. But sometimes a little bit of solitude and a kiss of nature is just what the soul needs.

TIP
ACRES controls other preserves in neighboring counties that are a short drive from Fort Wayne. You can find them all at acreslandtrust.org.

PRESERVES

Fogwell Forest
9630 Whippoorwill Dr.

Mengerson Nature Preserve
5895 Stellhorn Rd.

Bicentennial Woods
340 E Shoaff Rd., Huntertown, IN

Blue Cast Springs
21412 Bluecast Rd., Woodburn, IN

Cypress Meadow
14502 Zubrick Rd., Roanoke, IN

Fox Fire Woods
17868 Hull Rd., Leo-Cedarville, IN

GET YOUR (RACE) DUCKS IN A ROW
AT WEIGAND CONSTRUCTION DUCK RACE

Watching more than 18,000 colorful plastic ducks make their way down the river surely places the Weigand Construction Duck Race at the top of the list for one-of-a-kind events. Spectators can watch as the ducks are dropped into the river and then race (well, actually float) along the water to the finish line. The annual summer event is a fundraiser for the nonprofit Stop Child Abuse and Neglect (SCAN). You can purchase one of the ducks in the race. However, you will not be able to keep the cute toy, as each duck is rounded up and scooped up by a large net to be used again at next year's race.

Promenade Park
202 W Superior St., 260-421-5000
scanfw.org

RIDE THE RIVER
ON SWEET BREEZE

Learning about history has never been so relaxing. Docents on the Sweet Breeze riverboat, which is modeled after an 1840s canalboat, provide passengers with colorful stories, historic tales, and lore about the city, all while taking in the scenic sites on the waterway. The boat is named after the daughter of Chief Little Turtle, a well-known Native American military leader who lived and is buried in Fort Wayne. The boat, a faithful replica, is used to celebrate the city's three rivers, while helping riders understand the important role the waters played in the past and still play in Fort Wayne. Tours, which are 45 to 90 minutes long, happen every weekend from May through September.

Boarding happens at Promenade Park, 202 W Superior St.
Forfw.org

TIP
Reservations are required and should be made early, as tours fill up quickly.
260-420-3962, FWoutfitters.com

Greekfest
Photo courtesy of Visit Fort Wayne

CULTURE AND HISTORY

MEET WALT WHITMAN
IN AN ALLEY

What do poet Walt Whitman, a panda licking an ice cream cone, and bluebirds have in common? Well, nothing, really, except they are among colorful murals that have been placed on the sides of buildings in alleyways and corridors throughout the heart of downtown. Public art has exploded in the city, and additional works are added each year. You might just be inspired to create your own painting as you walk around looking at the colorful works by various artists—including some who are known worldwide. In the meantime, spend a day, or maybe two, tracking down all the street art and public sculptures. A map showing the location of each work is available from Art This Way, part of the Downtown Improvement District.

artthiswayfw.com

TIP

Grab a slice of pizza at 816 Pint & Slice, 816 S Calhoun Street, and maybe a beer, and hang out in the alley at Porch Off Calhoun. The space next to this hipster pizzeria has been turned into an outdoor living room, where diners can enjoy one of the many murals while eating, drinking, listening to music, and playing games.

TAKE A TOUR
OF AMISH COUNTRY

Just a short drive from Fort Wayne is the quaint town of Grabill, which is heavily influenced by the Amish community. It's a place where it's not unusual to see horse-drawn buggies intermingle with modern-day vehicles along country roads. The small town offers a glimpse of a thriving Amish community, with picturesque farm scenes and unique shops. Most of the Amish community members shop and travel in Grabill, and often a horse and buggy can be seen parked outside a store. They also own businesses, giving visitors a chance to browse food, woodwork, and other products made locally. Since many of the Amish travel by buggy or bicycle, it's important to be aware of their presence when visiting Grabill.

MUST-SEE RECOMMENDATIONS:

H. Souder and Son's General Store
13535 Main St., 260-627-3994
A step back in time to an old country store, with flavored sodas, penny candy, and fudge in glass cases.

Country Shoppes of Grabill
13756 State St., 260-450-0115
150 antique and flea market vendors on two floors.

Grabill Country Sales
13813 Fairview Dr., (260) 627-8330
Amish-made bakery goods, along with other food and bulk items.

GET A HISTORY LESSON
AT OLD FORT

A trip to Fort Wayne wouldn't be complete without a visit to the city's reason for existing. The Old Fort is a replica of the original fort, which was located just a short distance away. The fort was ordered built by General "Mad" Anthony Wayne, the city's namesake. The historic site offers visitors a glimpse of what life was like during the 1800s. Buildings include enlisted soldiers' and officers' quarters, a blacksmith's shop, a hospital, and blockhouses. The fort grounds sit along the river, making the experience all the more authentic. Reenactment events happen regularly and feature reenactors dressed in authentic costumes, demonstrations of skills, and even the firing of a cannon. While the grounds are open year-round, the buildings are open only during events. There is no admission to the fort, and all the events are free.

1201 Spy Run Ave., (260) 437-2836
oldfortwayne.org

TIP

Say cheese! Take a selfie with the Gen. Anthony Wayne equestrian statue, located in Freimann Square downtown. The towering statue is a tribute to the city's founder.

HIT THE PITS
AT ARDMORE QUARRY

It may sound like one of those roadside attractions beckoning travelers with a sign that might say: "Hey, kids, come see the largest hole in the ground," but believe me, a drive to the Hanson Aggregates Mideast Ardmore Quarry is worth the trip off the beaten path. Standing on an observation deck that overlooks the work below, the public gets a chance to see workers mine limestone that is used to produce sand and gravel. The trucks and machinery look small in the quarry. Years of digging have created the massive, manmade mountain, as well as the giant earthen crater, which will amaze both the young and the old. The observation deck is open from daylight to dusk and is free.

4529 Sandpoint Rd., 260-478-9992

BE PRESIDENTIAL
WITH THE LINCOLN COLLECTION

Down below the main floor of the Allen County Public Library is one of the most overlooked and coolest collections the book repository oversees. The Lincoln Financial Foundation Collection is one of the world's most comprehensive collection of artifacts from our 16th president, Abraham Lincoln. Visitors can find photos, papers, letters, and even poetry from Lincoln and his family. Docents of the collection offer up information and stories, including whether a photo really shows the ghost of Lincoln standing behind his wife, Mary. All of it is in a climate-controlled and fireproof room for its protection. You are likely to learn more here than you did in your high school history class. The collection is often used by authors, scholars, TV producers, and others who study Lincoln.

Allen County Public Library
900 Library Plaza Dr., 260-421-1200
acpl-cms.wise.oclc.org/research/lincoln-collection

TIP

Take time to track down your family tree at the Genealogy Center, which also is located at the library. The center offers one of the largest family research collections in the country, including records from around the world. People come from all over the country to the center to conduct genealogical research.
260-421-1225
acpl-cms.wise.oclc.org/genealogy

APPRECIATE GREAT ART
AT FORT WAYNE MUSEUM OF ART

Visitors can stroll past artwork from the 19th century to today at the Fort Wayne Museum of Art. The mid-size museum, which opened in 1921, focuses on American art and offers permanent and temporary exhibitions that pull from the thousands of art items it has collected over the years, as well as from national traveling exhibitions. Artwork in the collection includes everything from Indiana Impressionism to glasswork by Dale Chihuly. Bonus: there is even art outside, with sculptures and metal pieces that were made especially for the museum. The museum offers free admission every Thursday from 5 to 8 p.m., and visitors can learn more about the artwork with a free curator's tour the first Thursday of the month.

311 E Main St., 260-422-6467
fwmoa.org

TIP

Take home your own piece of art at the museum's Paradigm Gallery. The shop offers pieces of work from local, regional, and national artists in different media. You also can see artists demonstrate their work on the second Thursday of each month.

SEE "AWESOME" AFRICAN-AMERICAN HISTORY
AT AAAHSM

The African/African-American Historical Museum (AAAHSM) is home to the city's largest public collection of African art and exhibits the histories of people of African descent in Allen County since 1809. AAAHSM, or "Awesome" as it calls itself, gives visitors a chance to see how African Americans helped shape the city and the important roles they played in its development. Guided tours are offered of this often-overlooked museum, which is housed in an older, two-story, Victorian-style home built in the 1890s. There are many exhibits, artifacts, photos, and clippings available to explore throughout the museum. Items include a bust of the Rev. Martin Luther King Jr., created by sculptor Will Clark; the NFL jersey of Hall-of-Famer and Fort Wayne son Rod Woodson; and photos of the city's first Black policeman and policewoman.

436 E Douglas Ave., 260-348-4465

TIP
The museum is open by appointment only.
Potential visitors can call and schedule a time for a guided tour.

SEE ARTWORK
IN AN OLD STONE CASTLE

There are no fairy princesses or dragons in this downtown castle, but it does house amazing artwork and antique furnishings any art lover should see. Now home to the Castle Gallery, the mansion, which is more than 100 years old and made of giant, granite boulders, was once home to the Fort Wayne Museum of Art and is on the National Register of Historic Places. It is a romantic spot for a date night, as couples can wind their way through the maze of artwork from local, regional, and national artists. One of the museum's more romantic exhibits is its annual Valentine's show. The museum is open limited days and hours, but appointments can be scheduled and the staff is always willing to show off the unique gallery and historic home.

1202 W Wayne St., 260-426-6568
castlegallery.com

TIP
The museum is free, but a donation is requested.

DIG FOR FOSSILS
AT FOX ISLAND

Those looking for an adventure or maybe just wanting to add to a collection can spend some time digging for prehistoric finds in Fox Island County Park's fossil pile. While you may not dig up a dinosaur, your chances finding a sea creature such as a prehistoric brachiopod are good. The pile is refreshed regularly with sediment donated by a local aggregate company and is turned over each spring. There isn't much prep required except to pick a spot and start digging. The fossils are perfect souvenirs for a budding paleontologist. It should be noted that there is a $2 fee per person for ages seven and older to get into the park, but it doesn't cost anything to pocket the fossils you find once you are in.

7324 Yohne Rd., 260-449-3180
allencountyparks.org

TIP
Dirty from all that digging? You can rinse off in the park's natural swimming hole. The pond, called Bowman Lake, is a perfect place to go in the summer and offers a small beach for lounging. There also is a Doggie Beach where dogs can be off their leashes.

DANCE THE NIGHT AWAY
WITH THE BALLET

The Fort Wayne Ballet is a shining star in Fort Wayne's art and cultural community. The professional dance company offers regular performances of classical and contemporary dances that show off its elegant and talented dancers, who come from around the area and around the world. The organization is the only professional ballet company in Indiana, and you quickly see why it has lasted so long after watching a performance. One of its most beloved and popular performances is *The Nutcracker*, which quickly sells out each December. The show has become a family tradition for many and is a holiday favorite. The ballet makes its home in the Arts United Center, located on the Downtown Arts campus, but it performs on several stages and at different locations.

300 E Main St., 260-484-9646
fortwayneballet.org

TAKE
A HISTORICAL WALK
ON HERITAGE TRAILS

You can explore the historic aspects of Fort Wayne on your own with Architecture & Community Heritage's (ARCH) Heritage Trails. ARCH, a historic preservation organization, offers four different trails throughout the city, all of which feature unique points of interest. Each trail stop is within walking distance of one another, and each landmark has a marker providing information about the site. You can read the markers or listen to the information by scanning a QR code with your smartphone. There are 59 stops in all, and many lead walkers to some of the most iconic spots within the city. But the best one for getting a feel of downtown history is probably the Central Downtown trail. The trail offers 19 stops and leads to such spots as the courthouse, Lincoln Tower, The History Center, the city's last two forts, and the Nickel Plate Railroad.

260-426-5117
archfw.org

TIP
Keep in mind that this is a self-guided walking tour,
so you will want to wear comfortable shoes and bring sunscreen.

HAIL A TRAIN
AT BAKER STREET STATION

Not much has changed at the Baker Street Station (formerly the Pennsylvania Station) since it first opened its doors in 1914—except, of course, that there are no longer trains coming and going. History buffs will enjoy seeing the station that was the major gateway for those coming to Fort Wayne and was a whistle-stop for every US president, from Harding to Eisenhower. The building is listed on the National Register of Historic Places for its mixture of classical and medieval elements, such as large arched windows, barrel-vaulted concourse, oak woodwork, and terrazzo and green-veined marble flooring. Visitors to the concourse will feel like they are waiting for the next train, and may even be able to hear a whistle blowing in the distance.

221 W Baker St., 260-749-1162
bakerstreettrainstation.com

TIP
The building is now used as a banquet space and offices,
but it is open to the public during office hours.

A FESTIVAL YOU BUSK SEE
ALONG DOWNTOWN STREETS

It's been said a mime is a terrible thing to waste, so it's a good thing they will always have a place at Buskerfest. The annual summer event is a celebration of the art of street performing. Buskers, including live statues, fire-eaters, acrobats, jugglers, dancers, musicians, and fortune-tellers, take up residence along Calhoun and Wayne streets to showcase their unusual talents. While many of the performances are planned, there are sure to be some that are not, as performers tend to make their way to the festival and do their own thing where they can. It's just another reason why the festival, which has been going on for more than 10 years, has created its own niche among city events. Buskerfest is free, but the buskers do accept gratuities.

downtownfortwayne.com/buskerfest

EXPLORE THE GRAVESITES
AT LINDENWOOD CEMETERY

Visiting a cemetery probably isn't high on your list of recreational activities. However, a visit to the Lindenwood Cemetery may just change your mind. The cemetery offers a peaceful respite from the hustle and bustle of downtown life and is steeped in city history. The 175-acre cemetery, listed on the National Register of Historic Places, offers beautiful gardens, mature trees, and a serene atmosphere. Some of the city's most famous residents can be found at Lindenwood. It was established in 1859, and graves from the city's first cemetery were relocated there after the original became overcrowded. Many of the founding fathers of Fort Wayne are at Lindenwood, as are hundreds of Civil War veterans. In all, Lindenwood contains more than 70,000 graves.

2324 W Main St., 260-432-4542

TIP

It is true that all of the graves from the city's original cemetery were moved to Lindenwood—all but one. The grave of Indiana's seventh governor, Samuel Bigger, is still located in McCulloch Park because his family could not be located to get approval for his relocation. There is a memorial at the park marking the gravesite. 1330 McCulloch St., fortwayneparks.org

---

LIGHT UP THE HOLIDAYS
WITH SANTA

It wouldn't be the holidays without the Big Guy, and each year his appearance brightens downtown. Thousands gather for the annual Night of Lights on Thanksgiving eve to watch the lighting of Santa and his reindeer, officially kicking off the holiday season. It's a tradition that began in the 1930s when the former Wolf & Dessauer Department Store first introduced the Santa display. Now, the restored Santa in his sleigh, pulled by the reindeer, hangs on the side of the PNC Center, offering both young and old a glimpse of a bygone era. Generations of families make the yearly visit to the Santa lighting, including grandmas and grandpas who watched the lighting when they were kids and are now sharing it with their grandchildren. It's no doubt a representation of a community's holiday spirit.

Main St. near Calhoun St.
downtownfortwayne.com

TIP

Santa isn't the only lighting display that comes to life on this night. There are several other light displays that are placed on buildings throughout downtown. Families can make a night of traveling from lighting to lighting, culminating with Santa's illumination.

JOIN THE FAITHFUL
AT THE CATHEDRAL

Fort Wayne is known as the City of Churches. One of downtown's most elegant and historic churches is the cathedral of the Immaculate Conception. Built in 1860, the Cathedral boasts Gothic-style architecture, Bavarian stained-glass windows, vaulted ceilings, and wood carvings. The structure is just as breathtaking outside as it is inside, and contributes to the downtown skyline. The church is the primary cathedral for the Roman Catholic Diocese of Fort Wayne-South Bend. Mass is offered daily and on the weekends. The cathedral is open daily for visitors. Interestingly, a crypt where some of the diocese's bishops are entombed lies beneath the cathedral, and the grave of the last Miami Indian chief, Joseph Richardville, can be found in the cathedral cemetery. Guided tours of the cathedral are available, but must be arranged at least one day before your planned visit.

1102 S. Clinton St., 260-424-1485, ext. 302

TIP

Take some time to explore the Diocesan Museum, which explores the history of the diocese of Fort Wayne-South Bend and includes a treasure trove of relics, paintings, statues, and Bibles, including one that dates to the year 1250. Admission to the museum is free and will appeal to both Catholics and non-Catholics. The museum is open 10 a.m. to 2 p.m. Tuesday through Saturday.
1103 S Calhoun St.

TAKE A PAGE FROM THE HISTORY BOOK
AT THE HISTORY CENTER

It won't come a shock that what you'll find at the History Center is, well, history. What you may not know is that the museum, once the home of the old City Hall, is a repository for more than 32,000 unique artifacts, photos, and documents that tell the rich heritage of Fort Wayne and Allen County. However, don't think this is some stuffy museum; many of the exhibits are designed to take you back in time, such as when the gas pump and television were invented (both in Fort Wayne). As you're exploring the museum, make sure to head to the basement, where the old city jail was located until 1971. The jail is hidden in the bowels of the building, allowing visitors to step inside the cells where those who were arrested years ago were locked up.

302 E Berry St., 260-426-2882
fwhistorycenter.org

TIP

The History Center also operates the Chief Richardville House, recognized as the oldest Native American structure in the Midwest. The home belonged to Chief Jean Baptiste de Richardville, whose mother was a Miami Indian. The home is open the first Saturday of the month from May through October.
5705 Bluffton Rd.

LET US ENTERTAIN YOU:
EMBASSY THEATRE

The Embassy Theatre is one of the few entertainment palaces that have survived for more than 90 years. A true cinematic treasure, it opened as a movie house in 1928 and was dressed to impress with ornate decorations, marble floors, columns, and a mezzanine. It has since hosted many big-name entertainers, from Bob Hope, Louis Armstrong, and Cab Calloway to today's concerts, touring Broadway shows, and the Fort Wayne Philharmonic. The theater even comes with its own friendly ghost. Visitors may catch a glimpse of Bud Berger, the longtime stage manager who lived and worked at the theater before his death in 1965. It could be that the empty seat next to you is already taken.

125 W Jefferson Blvd., 260-424-6287
fwembassytheatre.org

TIP
Catch a performance with the Grande Page Pipe Organ, which is one of only two pipe organs in the country at their original locations. The organ accompanies many movies shown at the Embassy, including a series of silent films, hearkening back to the theatre's earliest days.

STEP BACK IN TIME
AT THE JOHNNY APPLESEED FESTIVAL

Every fall, visitors can return to the 1800s at the Johnny Appleseed Festival. The festival is unique, as vendors are required to dress in 1800s period dress and no modern conveniences are allowed. Even the food, including those giant turkey legs and caramel corn, must be cooked over an open fire. Reenactors offer demonstrations of trades and skills as they existed during that time. The best part is that admission is free, which is a good thing, since you'll want to save your money for shopping the more than 200 booths. Another festival tradition is bringing an apple and tossing it on the grave of Johnny Appleseed, which sits atop a hill in the park where the festival takes place. It is believed that this is not the actual grave of John Chapman, the legendary pioneer who traveled around planting apple seeds, but you can pay tribute, anyway.

Johnny Appleseed Park
1502 Harry W. Baals Dr., 260-427-6003
johnnyappleseedfest.com

TIP

Parking is available for a fee at the Memorial Coliseum, near the festival, but free parking and a shuttle are available at several locations. You can find them by visiting the website.

VISIT
A FIREFIGHTER HOT SPOT

You can't slide down the fireman's pole, but you can see what it was like to be a city firefighter more than 100 years ago at one of the earliest fire stations in the city. The Fort Wayne Firefighters Museum is in the former Engine House #3, which was built in 1893. Visitors can see displays of a steamer that was pulled by horses, 1920s fire engines, and other items that were used by the Fort Wayne Fire Department. The building became the largest firehouse in the city and was retired in 1972 after a new, modern fire station was built. The museum is a unique destination to see how the Fort Wayne Fire Department transformed from a volunteer department beginning in the 1800s to paid professionals today.

226 W Washington Blvd., 260-426-0051
fortwaynefiremuseum.com

TIP
The museum is closed on Wednesdays and Sundays.
You can either walk in or schedule a tour by calling ahead.

EXPLORE
THE LANDING

The Landing in downtown Fort Wayne is where it all started for the city. This historic spot was the location of the Wabash and Erie Canal, where boats would land for trading, which is how it got its name. Since the 1800s, the area along Columbia Street has been a commercial hub, making it the busiest place in town. Now, the canal is gone, and there is different trading that goes on. The historic area has been revitalized and offers shopping, restaurants, and a spot for festivals and events. The renovations have given the area a new life and vibrancy, making it once again the place to be downtown. The street is closed to traffic, which makes it perfect for exploring one of downtown's oldest but newest spots.

100 block of W Columbia St.

TIP

Parking is a little hard to come by around The Landing. There is metered parking along Calhoun, Harris, and Pearl streets, and a nearby parking garage.

GET CULTURED
WITH DIVERSE FESTIVALS

Fort Wayne is a city of diverse cultures, and the best evidence of this are the immigrants who settle here and the festivals that celebrate their heritage. Beginning in spring and extending through summer, festivalgoers can enjoy a different cultural festival almost every weekend. There are longtime festivals such as Germanfest, which celebrates the long German heritage in the city, along with newer ones like Arab Fest and Fiesta Fort Wayne, which highlights the growing Hispanic community. With so many events to choose from, you pretty much have your summer social calendar mapped out once you get here. Whether you are a visitor or resident, embrace the culture by enjoying the food, music, and activities the festivals offer. Opa!

FESTIVALS

Cherry Blossom Festival at the Allen County Public Library
900 Library Plaza

cherryblossomfw.com

Arab Fest at Headwaters Park
333 S Clinton St.

arabfestfw.com

Germanfest at Headwaters Park
333 S Clinton St.

germanfest.org

Greekfest at Headwaters Park
333 S Clinton St.

fortwaynegreekfestival.org

Three Rivers Festival, featuring International Village at Headwaters Park
333 S Clinton St.

threeriversfestival.org

Fiesta Fort Wayne at Headwaters Park
333 S Clinton St.

SHOPPING AND FASHION

GET FASHIONABLE
AT THE VERA BRADLEY SALE

A girl can never have too many purses or accessories! If you don't agree, then you have never been to the Vera Bradley outlet sale. The annual sale celebrates accessorizing, as it offers an opportunity to score some great fashion finds at reduced prices. Vera Bradley is headquartered in Fort Wayne and is known for its beautiful, quilted patterns and styles on just about everything. Vera Bradley items are often seen on the arms of the famous and not-so-famous. The spring sale has become a spot for a girlfriend's getaway or mother and daughter shopping, drawing thousands of people each year. And while there are a number of good deals, $3,500 is the limit a person can spend during the five-day event.

Sale happens at Memorial Coliseum
4000 Parnell Ave.
verabradley.com

TIP

If you do plan to shop, you must register for the sale. Even after registering, you should still plan to wait in line, as only a limited number of people are allowed inside at a time because of fire codes.

ATTAIN
BOOK LOVERS' NIRVANA
AT HYDE BROTHERS

At Hyde Brothers Booksellers, bibliophiles can spend hours searching more than 150,000 used books that are stacked from floor to ceiling on two floors, including the basement, in this cozy, independent bookstore. Hyde Brothers has become a repository for odd and obscure titles. You can bet you won't find many of these titles at the corporate bookstores. The staff is knowledgeable and can help you find whatever you are looking for. Or, if you don't know what you want, they can pick out books for you based on your interests, whether they be mystery, romance, philosophy, or adventure. Most of the staff-picked packages are named after four other staffers—cats whose duties seem to be prowling the stacks or taking naps in the middle of the aisles.

1428 Wells St., 260-424-0197
hydebros.com

TIP

Explore the mural of the city on the side of the building that houses the bookstore. Painted in 2009 by artist Julia Meek, the mural highlights attractions and businesses in downtown Fort Wayne.

SAMPLE FORT WAYNE'S GROWERS AND MAKERS
AT FORT WAYNE'S FARMERS MARKET

There is no better place to get a taste and feel for Fort Wayne than at its many farmers markets. Each spring, the markets open for business throughout downtown, aside from the two that are open year-round. The YLNI Farmers Market settles in for the summer along Barr Street in the heart of downtown. It offers an array of vendors with products including food, flowers, art, jewelry, and clothing, and features live music as well. During the colder months, it retreats into the former Aunt Millie's Bakery building, which offers a spacious layout for sellers and buyers. Of course, you never know what you will find at these markets, so don some comfy shoes and grab a few bags to carry your purchases while you walk and explore.

MARKETS

YLNI Farmers Market
Outside every Saturday from May through September
Corner of Barr and Berry streets
Indoors from October through April
350 Pearl St.
ylni.org

Fort Wayne's Farmers Market
Outside every Saturday from May through September
McCulloch Park
1795 Broadway Ave.
Inside every Saturday from October through May
Parkview Field concourse
285 W Douglas Ave.
ftwaynesfarmersmarket.com

South Side Farmers Market
Open every Saturday from May through December
3300 Warsaw St.
southsidefarmersmarket.com

Historic West Main Street Farmers Market
Open every Friday from May through October
1936 W Main St.

Salomon Farm Park Farmers Market
Open Wednesdays from June through early September
817 W Dupont Rd.

HAVE A FEW LAUGHS
AT STONER'S FUNSTORE

Stoner's Funstore's website is Funnygoofycrap.com, and why not? That's exactly what you'll find in this downtown shop, which offers gag gifts, funny jokes, costumes, makeup, and magic tricks. There are chattering teeth next to fake dog poop, exploding gum, fake teeth and wigs, and yes, even a rubber chicken. The store also is the go-to place for costumes, with a massive selection that you can buy or rent. And the magic section offers tricks for the beginner to the advanced magician, as well as items from the store's founder and longtime magician Dick Stoner, who is known for his performances in the city. Stoner's has been making people laugh since 1949, and you're sure to find something that will tickle your funny bone.

712 S Harrison St., 260-426-1100
funnygoofycrap.com

TIP
If you're lucky, you may be able to catch Dick Stoner performing magic tricks in the store. There's really not a schedule for when he comes in, but it's always a treat when he does.

RECLAIM HISTORY
AT A SALVAGE STORE

Fans of HGTV and those with a fondness for old things can spend hours browsing Reclaimed Fort Wayne. The shop offers items that have been salvaged from old homes—many of them historic and unique. You'll find everything from doors and doorknobs to windows, paintings, architectural decor, and fireplaces. Need a skeleton key? They have those, too. There are even items such as toy soldiers, china, cameras, and photo albums. You never know what will be available at the store, and new old stuff is always being added. The owners have a good handle on what they have and don't have, as they are the ones traveling to old homes that are about to be demolished to see what treasures they can save. Each item has its own story and is just waiting for a new purpose.

1514 St. Joseph Blvd., 260-244-8999
reclaimedfortwayne.com

TIP
The store is open only on Thursdays, Fridays and Saturdays.

STUFF YOUR STOCKING
AT DARLINGTON

Holiday shopping takes on a new meaning at Darlington Holiday Warehouse. You can spend quite some time browsing the many aisles filled with thousands of gifts—many for less than $5—that will suit anyone on your holiday list. There also are holiday decorations, wrapping paper and bows, and some of the best caramel corn around. Customers snap up bags of it. The store is locally owned and unique. It is in a spacious warehouse, and I am not kidding about how much stuff you can find there. It is open only from October through Christmas Eve. However, that just gives the holiday helpers time to prepare for Christmas next year.

615 W Coliseum Blvd., 260-482-1645
whatisdarlington.com

TIP
Keep in mind that all sales are final.

"MEAT"
AT THE NEIGHBORHOOD MARKET

There was a time when the only place people had to shop was the neighborhood market. The Pio Market is a throwback to that time. The Pio Market is an old-fashioned neighborhood butcher shop and grocery store that still looks like it did back in the 1920s. In the back of the store there is a little stool-lined mini-counter that faces the meat counter, and a refrigerated case filled with unique sodas. The shop is decorated with several old advertising displays, and there is even an old, crank-style telephone. Of course, the food items have changed since the market first opened, but the wood floors, soda cooler, and butcher counter are the same. The shop even has a section with penny candies—including tiny paper bags to place your candy in—that will make you feel like a kid again.

1225 E State Blvd., 260-484-5414

ENJOY
BOUTIQUE SHOPPING
DOWNTOWN

West Wayne and Berry streets downtown are a shoppers' bonanza, with cute and quirky boutique shops that span several blocks. Each store is unique in the items it offers, turning the experience into a shopping treasure hunt. Two of those special stores that have a larger mission are the Creative Women of the World and the Third World Fair Trade Shoppe. Both shops sell items from around the world, giving artisans in poor villages or impoverished areas a chance to sustain themselves through their works. Creative Women particularly focuses on women artisans, providing opportunities for them to become their own bosses to overcome poverty and human trafficking. The store provides city shoppers with an array of one-of-a-kind and beautiful products that are perfect as gifts or just something for yourself.

STORES

The Find
133 W Wayne St.
thefindfw.com

**First & Wilkerson
Designs**
127 W Wayne St.
firstwilkerson.com

**Creative Women
of the World**
125 W Wayne St.
gocwow.org

Smiley's Joy
503 W Wayne St.
smileysjoy.com

David Talbott Collection
532 W Berry St.

Urban Hippie
534 W Berry St.
theurbanhippie.biz

Fancy and Staple
1111 Broadway
shopfancyandstaplefw.com

The Hanger Boutique
537 W Jefferson Blvd.
facebook.com/TheHangerBoutiq-
ueFTW

Idlehour
526 W Jefferson Blvd.
idlehourboutique.com

**Third World Fair Trade
Shoppe**
611 W Wayne St.
thethirdworldshoppe.com

ACTIVITIES
BY SEASON

WINTER

Walk through the Gardens at Foellinger-Freimann Botanical Conservatory, 39

Visit Old Saint Nick on the Santa Train, 55

See Holiday Creations at Festival of Gingerbread, 59

Ice Out, Baby: Headwaters Ice Skating, 66

Chill Out with Komets Hockey, 73

Sit Courtside with Mad Ants Basketball, 72

Dance the Night Away with the Ballet, 102

Light Up the Holidays with Santa, 107

Stuff Your Stocking at Darlington, 126

Listen to the Classics with the Fort Wayne Philharmonic, 46

SPRING

Eat, Walk, and Talk with Fort Wayne Food Tours, 13

Go Wild at Fort Wayne Children's Zoo, 37

Play Ball: Fort Wayne TinCaps Baseball, 62

Stop and Smell the Roses at Lakeside Park, 74

Get Fashionable at the Vera Bradley Sale, 120

Chill Out at Zesto Ice Cream Stand, 22

SUMMER

FALL

SUGGESTED
ITINERARIES

FAMILY TIME

Ice Out, Baby: Headwaters Ice Skating Rink, 66

Get The Wheel Deal: Wooden-Floor Roller-Skating, 78

Go Wild at Fort Wayne Children's Zoo, 37

Walk through the Gardens at Foellinger-Freimann Botanical Conservatory, 39

You Glow, Girl (or Boy) at Crazy Pinz, 57

See A Summer Haze of Sunflowers at the Farm, 83

Get Your (Race) Ducks in a Row at Weigand Construction Duck Race, 86

Hit the Pits at Ardmore Quarry, 95

Dig for Fossils at Fox Island, 101

Light Up the Holidays with Santa, 107

Have a Few Laughs at Stoner's Funstore, 124

Eureka! Experiment at Science Central, 44

Be a Holy Roller at Most Precious Blood Church Bowling Alley, 42

SHOPPING EXPERIENCE

Get Fashionable at the Vera Bradley Sale, 120

Stuff Your Stocking at Darlington, 126

"Meat" at the Neighborhood Market, 127

Enjoy Boutique Shopping Downtown, 128

Attain Book Lovers' Nirvana at Hyde Brothers, 121

Reclaim History at a Salvage Store, 125

Have a Few Laughs at Stoner's Funstore, 124

CULTURAL ATTRACTIONS

FOODIE SPOTS

PLACES TO IMBIBE

FREE TO ME

OUTDOOR ADVENTURES

ROMANCE IN THE CITY

Clip-clop through the City with a Carriage Ride, 52

Feel Amore at Italian Connection, 31

Stop and Smell the Roses at Lakeside Park, 74

See Artwork in an Old Stone Castle, 100

Walk through the Gardens at Foellinger-Freimann Botanical Conservatory, 39

See the Stars at the Observatory, 54

SWEET TREATS

Partake of Confection Perfection at Debrand Fine Chocolates, 10

Go Back to the Future at Rusty's Ice Cream, 33

Get Your Geek on at Sweets So Geek, 25

Savor the Flavor of Cupcakes at Zinnia's, 19

Take Sweet Notes at West Central Microcreamery, 20

Sip Handmade Sodas and Floats at Lincoln Tower Soda Fountain, 7

Chill Out at Zesto Ice Cream Stand, 22

HISTORY LESSON

Ride the River on Sweet Breeze, 87

Get a History Lesson at Old Fort, 94

Step Back in Time at the Johnny Appleseed Festival, 113

Be Presidential with the Lincoln Collection, 96

Take a Historical Walk on Heritage Trails, 103

Hail a Train at Baker Street Station, 104

Explore the Gravesites at Lindenwood Cemetery, 106

Join the Faithful at the Cathedral, 108

Take a Page from the History Book at the History Center, 110

Visit a Firefighter Hot Spot, 114

Explore the Landing, 115

INDEX